G000074957

ODD BOY

Odd Boy
Copyright © 2019 by Martin Jude Farawell

Cover photograph provided by author

Cover design by Seth Pennington

Author photograph by Mark Hillringhouse

All rights reserved. No part of this book may be reproduced or republished without written consent from the publisher, except by reviewers who may quote brief excerpts in connection with a review in a newspaper, magazine, or electronic publication; nor may any part of this book be reproduced, stored in a retrieval system, or transmitted in any form, or by any means be recorded without written consent of the publisher.

Sibling Rivalry Press, LLC
PO Box 26147
Little Rock, AR 72221

info@siblingrivalrypress.com

www.siblingrivalrypress.com

ISBN: 978-1-943977-67-3

Library of Congress Control No: 2019942241

By special invitation, this title is housed in the Rare Book and Special Collections Vault of the Library of Congress.

First Sibling Rivalry Press Edition, October 2019

ODD BOY

MARTIN JUDE FARAWELL

SIBLING RIVALRY PRESS

DISTURB/ENRAPTURE

LITTLE ROCK, ARKANSAS

FOR CHERYL

Contents

FOUR

FIVE: GENESIS: A Sequence of Poems

I am trying to learn: time suffered
is not necessarily time destroyed.

– Galway Kinnell

ONE

The Pine Barrens

1.

A rope hangs from a branch
too thin for a man's weight,
bent midway over a stream only
a very small boy would call a river
and think it fun to swing and drop
through such shallow water.
Under the foothold knot
it's frayed thistle-delicate,
and only those white hemp hairs move,
as a thistle's do,
in any moving air,
while the water-heavy rope
stays in unswaying plumb.
I don't test it.
Know my bones' frailty has grown
big as my body.

Downstream, a clay-colored log, its almost-canoe
halved bark, upturned under it, bridges
the narrowest, steepest gap.
The trunk, peat-soft, too wet to crack,
makes wrung sponge sounds as it breaks
slowly with my weight, so slowly
I've time to walk across.

The boy who hung that rope
could not have dragged this here.
There must have been many of them,
teasing and daring each other,
riding hard on bicycles to come this far,
far from that odd boy, with the sullen eyes

they avoided. And I, that
odd boy, come to the clearing, deer
tentative, watching from the trees, wanting
to run forward, to dare and swing.

2.

Heat-squashed beer cans, undersides carbon-black,
some flaked down to rust-fragile rims,
and brown and green bottles, bottoms
broken off in perfect circles, necks
snapped, mouths shattered,
litter every path and rock outcrop.

In the center of this circle of debris,
a smaller, burnt circle, site of many fires
kindled, re-kindled, until what was
new wood, dead wood, blackened,
re-blackened, into one burn
ringed with boulders and stumps
generations of hunters, or
perhaps, teenagers carried here
to laugh, drink, brag, and
maybe, if it grew dark enough
and they got drunk enough,
sing.

I step around the burn, remember
standing outside the circle
of other people's singing, of arms
embracing shoulders, and retreating
into the dark wood, thinking
how lovely their voices sounded
from a distance. Remember
Brian and my brother smuggling
Boone's Farm Apple Wine into the woods

and I, excluded, drunk from single shots
of bourbon, scotch, vodka filched
from my father's liquor cabinet,
vomiting in my room. Remember
my father's kiss, his alcoholic breath
breathed into my body. Remember
being so aware of my body, of its
smallness under the bed, as I shrunk
from his crashing into furniture,
crashing into my mother
another child, another child that would wish
it could shrink to invisibility. Remember
drunken singing ends
in breakage.

3.

"Bob Loves Darlene '68"
darkens where it's gouged
in the gray oak's side.
That was the year
my Uncle Frank, who taught me
to tell direction by stars, weather by wind
and cloud height, which prints meant jack-rabbit,
muskrat, raccoon or buck, began
to die. He who taught me
the way of gentleness, the way
of the deer, of that patience which stills
and waits for what in the silent wood—
if one were patient and still enough—
might come alive. I was walking
my awkward, unbalanced act
between boy and man
when he went.
Would he have loved the teenager,
penknife in hand, poking

at a tree trunk, deciding, after all,
not to carve his name beside the name
of the girl he was in love with.
Who carved, only once, on the pier
where he'd sat all night, his name
and the date he did not drown himself.
Who kept coming back, as its edges
softened under footfalls, as the plank
crumbled with dry-rot, to look down,
and read it, and say, "I'm still here."
Would he have guided my carving hand
and said, "Carve her name big,
and between your names, no ampersand,
carve the word, 'loves'."

4.

A Navy jet tears so low over the clearing
I can see each separate seam
in its wings and doors.
Seconds after, its distorted scream
shrills with such force my legs shake.
I know now why they name their fighting jets
for carnivores, know they want them to scream,
to turn their enemies into children,
into panicking animals. And remember
the screams hurtled at me, the hands,
hangers, belts, switches, that panicked me
to animal. And here, on this
last day of spring, in these woods
suddenly terrified into silence, I begin
to cry.

I cannot be a fighting man,
so afraid of failing those who need me
that I beat them back, beat them most

when they most need, until I've taught anyone
who might ask anything of me, not
to ask. I cannot be an angry man,
so lonely, who knew touch
would hurt, who was so angry that he was
so easily hurt, he punished his loneliness out,
punished its boundaries out
into everyone, until everyone
who might have known him, knew
his loneliness instead.

It is the gentle men I want
to be remembered in me,
Frank, Jerry, Russell, Harry,
the first men who taught me
I could learn other than fear
from a man, whose hands
on my hands
gentled me toward knowing
the man I would be
would not be
my father.

5.

I have always stepped silently, like a deer
who freezes at a twig's break,
who holds still long enough
to be mistaken for a tree.

I wanted to be mistaken
for a tree,
one you could lean against
and know
it was too strong
to give.

But I did give.
Was peat soft,
too soft to crack,
made only spongy
wringing sounds
when I broke.

In the heavy air,
the insistent, mournful cry
of a hawk:

Why?

Why?

No answer.
Only the dry clack
of grasshoppers,
looking like shreds of ash
taken wing.

6.

A deer steps out onto my path,
a young buck, his antlers
thumb-length stubs, velvety, rounded.
He does not freeze or run, must know
it is too late for him, but stands
not three yards down the trail,
left ear twirling, head cocked,
watching me stand watching him.
And then he bows, three times, slowly,
as if to display the antlers
he knows will be his.
Whether he learned this
from watching older bucks

before they charged,
or if it's his acknowledgment
of my right to pass, I do not know, but
bow back, slowly, three times,
and when I'm done, he walks away
calmly, his gray fur merging
with the gray woods.

7.

Sometimes I wish I could walk away
forever from this world, then remember
I almost did, and want to walk
forever toward it.
But I don't know how.
My skills are those of an animal
who bolts. I have learned the deer's leap
is perfected in animal terror,
that won't look back at what it flees from,
and so, flees everything.
I stop. Look back: a trail of rusted
and broken debris.

There is no way out
of this human world
I walk away from,
no way out of this human body
that must carry me everywhere, except
to die.

I am still that boy
who did not swing from anything,
who stood on the edge
of other people's singing.
I was lying when I said
I have grown

to know my frailty;
I knew that
when a boy.

8.

A wind, tasting of rain, shushes
the trees. All at once, the dark leaves
pale, and ash scatters from generations
of dead fires, is carried to standing water
under a gray oak
where lovers
who dared name each other
can still, twenty years after,
name themselves
one who loved.

The rain comes.
What is burnt
surrenders
to the work of water.

I must begin
the long hike back
to where I first entered these woods
as a boy, and bring
a deer's attentiveness
to this human life.
I don't know how to live
with the memories I carry
or fill that place
where my fear is
unless I can carve my name
as a lover's
that weeps
as it names
those I love.

TWO

High Sierras

Sometimes silence
is wind,
the massing of air
between your body
and all the bodies
you were too hesitant
to touch.

Berkshire Mountains

1.

Even the birds are still
in this still
before storm air,

the only sound
a tick
as pine needles drop

thick on the forest floor.
Let me
be this green

until I fall, and my fall
as calm
and quick.

2.

So much time I wish
were silence,
as if in silence
I could find the life
the noise of life
invades.

So many hours I wish
were over,
so I could find the time
for the life I'd reach
if I had time
to go there.

In that life,
there is time
for all I've neglected
to repair,
all the tiny acts
of cowardice, and closing.

In that life,
my body
is never off-balance,
no part held back
from those
who would hold me.

3.

But I am dying
in this life,
where I hesitate to give

the greenest parts of me, afraid
that what is clipped and offered
won't come back.

I have seen the offering in faces
close
when I would not take,
in careful hands,
the green gifts
offered me.

The words I mean
yellow and fall
between the words I say
in layers of silence,
hot-house dank.

In the hesitant fall
of my hands
from those
who will fall
from me,
my life closes.

Whatever is not
opening,
curls back
in itself,
a white,
underground thing.

4.

I would sing
but my music
is a music
of pause,
and hesitation's
gaps
cannot be sung.

When senses hum,
body keens,
spirit shouts, we
must hum, keen, shout,
but the swallowed cry
makes only a sound
of swallowing.

I am sick with swallowed cries,
sick with fear
of being broken open
by what I can't
keep down,

as if any act of opening
were an act of violence.

If we could listen
close enough,
we'd hear
that even new shoots
scream.
It is this screamed song of birth
I want
the song of sudden opening.

Casino Pier, Asbury Park

I lift the child
onto the carousel.
Gripping horse
between hands and thighs,
he smiles, unafraid.

This amazes me.

I stand back, wary,
mirroring the gape-mouthed beasts
with their eyes of wooden terror
and their suspended limbs
of silent, desperate exertion.

The calliope heaves
its asthmatic tune,
blinking canopy lights
counting the cadence
of this surreal brigade
as they turn
and march away.

I am the intruder
in a world suited only
to children, to imaginations
not yet corrupt
with nightmare.

The child waves, grinning.

For some unnamed reason
he seeks
my approval;

while I,
bolted to the floor,
garishly prance.

South Mountain

Yanked toward the river,
by spring slides
of mud
and mud-black snow,
with no roots, no bark, no branches,
scales of fungus down their lengths,
the gutted trunks gather
where nuthatches drill them
for insects
that furrow through their bodies
as if they were earth.

Here, the odor of decay
is pungent as sex.
No hot-house flowers
to perfume death,
only the sweet reek
of sudden moistening,
as if the excitable earth
could ache with us, knowing
our bodies break open,
musty and slick
as mushrooms on loam
enriched by our flesh.

Ocean Gate

Summers used to always smell like this
green stain of fern leaves rolled
to dark moisture between palms,
of soil that puckered open
where garden weeds were plucked
and shook loose from shaggy-rooted undersides,
of wet seining nets and creosoted piers,
of seaweed-tangled mussels at low tide,
of charcoal, citronella, and cat-tail smoke,
of oranges and iced coffee, and peaches in red wine.

Behind the slap of poker cards
against the table top,
and the jingle of penny jars,
crickets scritched their insect lust
as beetles and moths thrummed
at window screens,
and the one that got in pinged
against the light until it died.
After the long, droning day,
I'd crawl across creaking bed springs to lie
by the open window
where nightbirds called me and
called me

and first up at first light,
I'd wander the woods until noon,
with a bucket for wild blueberries that grew
just beyond the border
of brambles and thorn bushes
that scraped beaded blood paths
across my knees and calves.
Returning to the faces

that had worried away the morning,
I'd lift up the bucket,
heavy with harvest,
and be forgiven for not being lost
but only gone blueberry picking.

But I was lost.
Lost and wandering after
whatever it was
that scritched at the screens,
that thrummed in panic
against my body,
desperate to get in,
more desperate
to get out,
something—there was so much
I wanted then,
I didn't know what,
only knew
the need to go
where I could be most
alone, under the guise
of blueberry picking,
where I had first heard,
and only if alone
would hear again,
the silence that would tell
what I listened for.

I am still wandering into summer noons,
after old scents, old sounds, as if one
could open the past for me
and let me find the boy
who wanders there,
and take his hand, and lead him
to the secret place

of perfect wild berries,
where we pick, eat, laugh, know
fern scent, and bird cry,
and late fruit breaking
on our tongues.

On the Boardwalk in Seaside Heights

A woman in imitation gold
bangles sits in a webbed chair
and beckons, "Come in for a reading,"
with a streetwalker's insouciance,
knowing what she proffers is the chance
to cheat the inevitable,
to slip the bonds
of was, is, will be,
and pretend time is a still well
where we lave our tongues at will,
instead of this river of detritus,
where whatever falls from us is lost,
is more lost
the more we reach after.

Beneath a string of colored cellophane pennants
that rustle like crow wings,
the Salvation Army Band
barrumps and bahoos
obeisance to its Lord.
Amen is the polite "ahem"
of those whose lips
are permanently pursed
at what is animal in us,
who cannot say, "So be it"
to the blood of our animal birth,
blood surge in our animal parts,
blood and flesh sloshed off our bones.

A girl in a humid shirt,
her sex as crisp as apples,
intones invitations to a game of chance.
I keep my hands in my pockets,

fingering change, wonder
if I've spent my life
like an old lady with a roll of quarters
in a garish purse,
gambled off, bit by bit,
never risking anything that matters.

They slap their money on the painted counter,
stare as if staring
could conjure the one
that will pluck them out
from the logic of numbers,
the terrible logic
of random necessity.
But all the numbers that rattle past
the pointing hand
tick down
to that final cipher:
the "O," grateful or terrified,
"So this is the day."

> *Oh, let us not, oh, God,*
> *be papery wings*
> *storm-winnowed out*
> *of a dry dune,*
> *all the seagull*
> *crushed out of us.*
> *Oh, let our bones, dear God,*
> *not leech into seawash,*
> *siphoned by mollusks, our ribs*
> *the ribbed shell hinged*
> *over a jetting clam.*

The ghost of a girl in a summer dress
dances on the boardwalk
with sparklers in her hands,

winks
at my sudden self-consciousness.
If I were seventeen and it were Independence Day
I would—how I wish I had—no I wouldn't,
not even now, dance with her.

Happy

Q: Why did God make man?
A: God made man to know him, to love him,
and to serve him in this world,
and to be happy with him forever in heaven.
—*The Baltimore Catechism*

1.

The Buddha sees the infinite suffering of the world and must laugh,
and so must Vinny "the skinny guinea" Fillipone, who,
if someone tripped in Confirmation class,
would laugh so hard he'd shake like a scarecrow in a windstorm.
Fall down a flight of stairs? He'd be so spastic with laughter
he'd tumble down on top of you, near ecstatic with delight
at his own bumps and bruises. Draw blood? Forget it.
He'd have to clutch his crotch and run lock-kneed for the boys' room,
begging every being in the known and unknown universe
to stop, please stop, don't make him laugh.
And Father Burke never thought he was enlightened.

2.

"That's right, Jesus said to turn the other cheek.
But what's he say about some punk
who won't stop pickin' on you and your pals?"
We looked away as Father Burke
plugged Vinny's nose with Kleenex.
"Nothing.
Know why?
'Cause even Jesus understood
some people can't be reached with kindness.
You get hit once?
You let it slide.
You get hit twice?
You take the s.o.b. out back and clean his clock."

3.

When Father Mills (the cool priest, the one who smoked in class,
and let us watch his still-lit cigarette
tumble four stories to the sidewalk
and never hit anyone) came to give
us future altar boys special religious instruction,
we asked what we thought impossible questions
like, "If God can do anything,
can He make a wall too high for Him to climb?
'Cause if He can't build it, or can't climb over,
He can't do everything." He'd answer,
that we were thinking on an earthly plane
while the mind of God was boundless.
(Which Kevin McGuinty explicated for us as,
 "Nah, He can't do it.") When we asked,
"Can God sin? 'Cause if He's all good,
He can't do evil; and if He can't do evil,
He can't do everything," he asked us, "Can you
make a universe? A solar system?
A planet? How about a grain of sand?"

"Well, actually Father," Kevin began,
with an ostentatiously obsequious smirk
that signaled to the rest of us
he was about to out-smart a grown-up,
"once, me and Vinny Fillipone..."

"That's 'Vinny Fillipone and *I*.'"

"Once, Vinny Fillipone and *I*
were smashing cinderblocks..."

"That doesn't count.
That sand already existed.
I mean from nothingness.

Can you make a grain of sand from nothing?
No?
Not even one tiny grain?
Then how can you expect to comprehend the mind
that created everything, the entire universe?
You trying to think like God
is like an insect trying to think like you.
Once you've left this earth, if you ever get to heaven—
McGuinty—you'll understand,"
which was a Jesuit's way of saying,
"Shut up and drop dead,
you little bug."

During a Funeral

(or A Lapsed Catholic Struggles to Repress a Giggling Fit)

You know it's right to stay attentive,
to hold imagination back,
but you haven't changed, not much
in all the years since Father Burke admonished,
"God gave His only son for you, and you
can't give Him   One.   Small.   Hour?"
For once again, the lucent dove breaks free
from the tall, maudlin windows above the altar
and dive-bombs the heads of the bereaved
with perfect, stained-glass shits.

Don't laugh. You're too old for this.
Focus on how somber the youngest altar boy looks,
and how guilty. You remember that
straining under serious brows to not
stare at the widow, the big clumsy mess
grown-ups made
of weeping, how they fell
into each other, impossible to untangle
who was holding whom
against collapse,
until it seemed their sorrow was a beast
it took both their bodies to contain.

As, back in sixth grade,
when Carmella's father died,
and the whole class was force-marched
into the funeral, trying to look pious,
to not think, even this was better
than an hour of math.
Carmella. Whatever happened to
Carmella? Hazelnut skin, sweet,

swollen, already a Botticelli at twelve,
in the pew before you, as you stared at that sacred,
naked place between white collar and black hair,
unable to stand for communion, your sin rising
against the gray fly of your flannel trousers.

Don't think of sex. Why do you always
think of sex at times like this? Think,
instead, of her mother's face, how it shook
like water, and Kevin nudging you,
the instant you'd seen it: that great snot bubble blown
from her left nostril, big as a ping-pong ball,
and you, palms pressed against your cheeks,
trying to squeeze shut the giggling fit
Sister Mary Mark would surely beat you for,
as now, with finger and thumb, you pinch closed
the grin pushing at the corners of your mouth.

The priest is staring at you. He knows. Look
serious. Look him dead in the eye. Christ,
he's fat. So much for vows of poverty. Don't
be cynical. Maybe it's glandular. What's so funny
about that word? You see him naked, big
paste-white belly, dimpled knees, unused sex
swinging just like that censer. Now it takes
an entire hand to still your smile. Concentrate
on the sermon. Don't. He's too obviously pleased
with his own mixed metaphors. Remember the dead man,
what you loved about him: There was always
his wonderful sense of humor: dry wit and smoke
issuing from one corner of his mouth, a cigarette
tucked into the other. You can almost
hear him at your ear, muttering under
his breath, "Isn't gluttony one of the deadly
sins?" You should have known, even dead
he'd be sarcastic.

Think of pain.
Think of Sister Mary Mark beating you
and Kevin with a yardstick for laughing in church,
how she kept on with the splintered ends after
it broke, and still, you bit down on humiliation,
rose, pulled up your pants and returned to your seat,
relieved, even proud, she hadn't made
you weep. And even though you knew, if you
laughed now, she would call you back to break you,
blow by blow, however long it took,
all was lost when Kevin whispered
between clenched teeth, "I think she likes you."
As now, it takes both hands to hold back
your laughter, and you bow to hide your face,
your whole body shaking, and just when you're certain
everyone will know, you feel a hand
on your back, feel it reach
across your shoulders.

What is there to do, but accept
any act of kindness?
Maybe this is God: this infinite
human mercy. Maybe we're mistaken,
and the willows bent over the river
are doubled with laughter.

THREE

Why We Have Monsters

The raincoat is
eager for your throat. Did
reach. But not again.
It will wait, wait out
thirty years of raincoat
until again
you turn.

Your mother knows
she lies, as she steps
inside, as she smiles
from the closet:
"See?
See?
There's nothing."

A Child's Tale

You do
what you will
to my body.

My body
is too little
to stop you.

I will
will myself
away.

While I'm gone,
my body
will make hair, muscle.

When I want to come back,
my body
will not welcome me.

Everything I Need to Know
I Learned in Kindergarten

I sit
in the second-to-last seat
in the row
by the windows.
Teacher gives us each
a crayon,
a clean sheet
of construction paper,
says, we begin
with writing
our names.

The children
hunch over,
ignoring everything
but this naming.
I am the only one
no one's shown
my few pieces
of the alphabet.

She walks quietly
to my blank face,
blank paper.
Is kind.
Takes the crayon gently.
Asks my name. I am
the dumbest one in the room.

Another Night at the Fights

And then
a silence
of awkward forks grating
on china
and too eager quenching
of unfelt thirst
as cups and saucers clank
against the sleepy protocol
and a cube of meat inspected
on all six sides
and a single pea
systematically mashed
into green pulp
as each throat cleared
denotes another
hesitation
and then
sonny spills his milk

Duet

My father was predictable in his rages.
When the shadows in his eye sockets deepened
until the shadows took his eyes
and the skin above his jawline
was sucked gaunt against his teeth
as if he'd chew his own cheeks off
then I knew the fleshless death's head
that harrowed my sleep
was the skull behind my father's face
that hated him, hated his life,
that would bite my spine in half
if not for my magic gift
of invisibility.

       But it was she,
singing Rosemary Clooney in the kitchen,
fox-trotting with a colander of glistening green beans
who would snap
and the metal pot or frying pan,
the bread board or rolling pin
would leap into her fist and swing her
skirling toward me, too fast
for me to vanish, who beat
her music into my spine
until I sang.

Now and at the Hour of Our Deaths

My brother,
in the lower bunk,
feigning sleep,
and the close ceiling,
beyond which
God is,
always,
listening,
or not;
the wet insides of my ears
hearing an underwater language
groan and rumble
through the near wall,
and the night, the night
is the stomach of a whale
swimming me forever
from my home,
through loneliness
and loneliness,
where my mother's voice
begs my father's name,
my father's name, and
no   no
again   again
as my fingers
that smell
like the inside
of a fielder's glove
tell the rosary,
and no matter how I pray—
Oh, mother of God,
Oh, blessed among women—
there is no grace.

First Night

The first night
I pissed myself,
woke
under sopped sheets,
placed my body
between the hall light
and you
who were not
my parents
but robots sent
to kill us,
and waited for my shadow
to wake you,
how was I to know
fear of you
would cling wet
to my belly
all my life?

Hands

My father did not teach me to make anything
except myself, small as I was, smaller;
did not guide my hands toward any making,
except once, a carving knife at my wrists,
to make me handless.
I learned from him
the security of corners.

My father never spoke about his childhood,
except with his hands, with his
father's hands, that made him do
the child beggar's dance
for mercy, to the time of words
that sang him small,
too small to ever be loved by anyone,
even his sons, the sons
he would make dance
after anyone's love.

I let no dance floor at my wedding,
only a man with a slow guitar,
and still, whatever floor there was
became dance floor, and only me,
cornered in my fear,
not dancing.
When the wedding was over,
he hugged my wife, just drunk enough
to tell her that he loved her,
just loud enough
for me to hear.

My father, I wish I could go back
to kiss your childhood

and make it better,
kiss your child with the kindness
of this woman kissing me,
or, if not that, that the past
could be something
that only happens once.

But the past keeps happening in my hands
no matter how I ball them up
as if the blows they held could be stilled
if I could hold them hard enough,
or driven out, into the walls, the doors
I drive my hands into,
or driven into me,
better into my body than into my sons.
I will have no sons
made to dance
by these hands
I will cut off
before they make anyone dance after anything.

What Does Not Pass

I wanted to talk to you about that summer evening
when you came out onto the porch to ask
if everything was alright.
That was the summer I called you an asshole
and you did not hit me
with a willow switch or belt,
but with your fist.
I was sixteen years old.

I stood up.
We both realized
I was looking down
at you. This was the last time.
If you struck me again
I would strike back.

Don't pretend you don't remember this;
it was the first time you were afraid of me,
afraid you'd raised a son who'd turn toward you
the face you'd turned
toward your father,
and you backed down.

That was the year your father died
and you sat in the kitchen saying,
"I never knew him.
We were strangers until he was dying."
I wished I could mourn for you
but was too angry
you'd let the same thing happen
between us,
and wanted to ask how could you,
but had already learned
some questions don't pass
between the fathers and sons
in our family.

All this was behind us
when you stepped out onto the porch,
looking shy.
I'd been sitting out there for hours,
trying not to make any noise.
I turned my head so you wouldn't see I was crying
and whispered, "Everything's fine."
You tossed your cigarette out onto the driveway, turned,
and went back inside.

For years I blamed no one for my adolescence
because that help had been offered
and I'd refused it. But I'm older now
and know some questions need to be asked
more than once,
that a life's time is made up of moments, and in ours
you turned and carefully closed the screen door behind you.

Now I want to tell you what I was doing
sitting out there alone,
all those nights on the front porch
through the summer I was sixteen
I was seventeen I was eighteen,
I was trying to find a reason not to kill myself, and,
not finding any, was planning out
the most painless and efficient method.

For whose benefit is it
I don't wait until you're dying
to tell you this?
It was years before I found
I had reasons to not want to die.
None of them had anything to do with you.

Suffer Little Children

"It's like those out-of-body stories on TV,"
he says, "except I'd shoot out—bang!
—like that, and sideways, not straight up. I'd float
a little, but mostly I'd keep zooming back
until it was like looking through the wrong end
of a telescope. And I could watch them,
see myself, but feel nothing. That's how
I know we have a soul: I left my body."

My brother in the basement being beaten.
I'm on the landing, dancing in panicked
ecstasy—*It isn't me! It isn't me
down there!*—spastic with desperation
to leave my body, the stink of turpentine,
of damp cement, dragging me back inside
my body, where my sister tugs our mother
toward the cries in the cellar, and she answers,
"But you're the one who told."

"The hell of it is," she says, her voice on the edge
of breaking, "when I feel like this I know
it's theirs, not mine, it's their pain. We,"
her voice breaks. "We just had it beaten
into us." I turn to comfort her,
but cannot find her hands. It's so dark.
I say aloud, "I can do nothing to comfort
my sister." The shame of having said this
forces me awake.

Mrs. Reilly calls down from her window
that if we don't behave, Satan himself
will burst up through the ground and cart us off
to hell. We must look like three Little Rascals,

staring bug-eyed at the sidewalk cracks, because
she bursts out laughing, "I'm only pulling your leg!"
We're five, six, eight, already understand
that she can't know, to joke like that,
and we can't tell her.

My brother and his wife look rapturous, press all
their love into convincing me, come Judgment Day,
no one saved will suffer. But I could never leave
my body, and don't believe in Paradise.
I cannot step across a sidewalk crack
and not hear his tortured cries beneath me.
How could it not be eternal agony to know
I had abandoned even one I love to hell?

Jung Said

1.

Jung said the figures in our dreams are always
manifestations of the self, that each
embodies traits in us we fear or loathe
and manage to deny when conscious, but
imagination opens toward them when
not limited by will. Therefore, the womb-
like dark that buoys me in dreams of peace
is not a memory or vestige of
prenatal bliss, but a symbol for my own unknowing,
which, once I see surrender of control
as not a form of death, will nurture and
enrich my creativity. That woman
at work, whose girlish squeals set my teeth
on edge, who tests the limits of my patience
with her every sentence frag-
ment, who, last night, in dreams, was buck-naked,
bucking above me, shouting, "Through the shoot
my brahma bull! I'll ride you till the stands
are shaking!" isn't someone secretly
I long for. Rather, she suggests I must
confront my childhood fear of seeming stupid,
and only then will know the joy that comes—
no pun intended—from embracing every
aspect of the self. Of course, Jung could
be wrong. If not, then everything we live
is as we dream, and everyone we meet
is just some facet of ourselves made flesh.
What we feel for them is not what passes
between one person and another, but
what sparks across the corpus callosum.
We are alone in dreams forever. So-
lipsism gets boring, I know. Sleep. Sleep.
Poppies.

2.

Jung said our dreams are mythic landscapes where
we fight the battle of to be. Or not.
I'm losing, Carl. What's worse, not only in
my sleep. Awake, the shadows swarming up
the bedroom walls are bats, are beetles from
the crawl space, eating along the timbers
to get at me. They can't, unless I close
my eyes and fall asleep, and then they'll charge
so swiftly I'll be gone before there's time
to scream. If all the creatures massing there
could keep their own eyes closed, I would be fooled
eventually, would blame imagination
for shaping them from nothing but the dark.
But always one is over eager, just
as I'm about to doze, takes a peek,
and isn't quick enough to shut its eyes
before I've seen. All night, the darkness is
a dome of close-packed bodies, with scatterings
of eyes that blink like stars. To make
them disappear, I only need to make
myself a three-year-old, believe I'm three,
calling out, "Mommy, there are eyes
in the dark," believe this time she tip-toes to
my bed, warms my face with lullabies,
and will not leave until the night is soft
and scented as her cotton dress. She doesn't
beat me, doesn't say, "I'll give you reasons
to cry." She hasn't even learned that memory
is merciless. I need new myths old Carl,
I have been terrified into blank verse.

If I Sing

If I sing, I weep.
If I sing joy, even sing joy, I weep.
If I weep, if I weep, if cries splatter from me,
if I sputter snot and spit down my chin, my shirt, your shirt,
if I shake and shake until you fear I'll shake apart,
don't be afraid for me, don't be ashamed,
I will not break from this, will not die,
but from the lack of it, from the closing,
and I will not close, will not hide, will not deny
anymore the child I was who could not cry out,
and now that I can cry I will sing,
even if my song comes shoved out
on the snot and spit I swallowed not
to cry, I will sing, I will sing
my joy that I will not hide this joy I sing for
even if singing, I weep.

FOUR

Field Guides

What we do not speak of
returns
as the first songbirds do,
the Scarlet Tanager,
the Indigo Bunting
you love; hedges
ever closer
under cover of dead
thistle and milkweed; calls,
Here!
    No!
        Over
here!
all along the edge
of silences
that always return
as the first leaves do
to earth, the Yellow Birch,
the White Ash
I love; flicks
from dry mouth
to dry mouth
of empty pods
once rupturing with such seed
the meagerest breath
would loose them.

The Favorite Saints

My father sleeps
between Saint Martin
and Saint Jude,
a statue of each
on either nightstand
as they stood
by my mother's bed
when she died.

I went in
to say goodbye
and saw them there,
palms upturned
in supplication,
in despair,
the patron saints
of hopeless cases,
the inconsolable poor.

"You know," she said,
"you have always
been special to me."
"Yes," I said, lying.

In This Light

Three days old, Corinne Anna,
not asleep, but not quite waking
in my arms, half opens her large eyes—
all iris and pupil, unable to focus
in this new light—which roll back and close
and almost shake under soft domed lids,
her whole body sighing. And so my mother,
a day before dying, unable to lift her domed head
with its furze of baby hair, all cheekbones
and small mouth, opening, opening,
her eyes unlearning
to see in this light, saw me
for the last time, and I held her head
in the curve of my neck, my chin
on her shoulder, and cried
as I must have, for the first time,
in this very place, and felt her hand
on the back of my head,
and her body sighed.

Homeless

In late February
my failures line up
begging in the rain.
Not trusting
my empty palms
they follow after,
patting my pockets
for change.

Sanctum Sanctorum

Sometimes the closest
we can come
to prayer

is kneeling in the kitchen
to sponge away
the jam

tracked across the floor
by the children
we will

not we will not
not ever
beat.

Turning

So much of my life was lost in wanting
I didn't know what, only knew
my life would be all wanting,
wanting so much
to get out of the life I was in
I wanted to get out
of life,
wanting to believe
there was somewhere
where being alive
was something to love.

When my life turned, and I turned
toward knowing that somewhere
was here,
I wanted to go back,
to reclaim those years
from their sadness,
now that I wanted to live forever
and knew those years were lost forever.
Only their sorrow is still mine.

There are moments I forget
how sad I once was,
when it seems
I was always this man,
under these hands
that tell my body
she is still in love with me.

Still. I hold the word on my tongue,
the long l's lingering.
I am still in this world where I am loved.

And as I turn to her
the child I was
turns in his wanting
time to love this life enough
to even love the life
that brought him here.

Even Asleep

Even asleep your body answers,
pressing back
into the press
of hands,
your sadness
in the small of your back,
eased away
as the muscles ease.

Sometimes your hair
is full of mourning
I comb through with my fingers
and play
until it all comes loose.

Sometimes my hands can find
beneath the shadows of your face
whatever it is
that darkens there
and with
just touch
make it go.

But somewhere you have a sorrow
with all my body
I cannot reach,
and then you hug me into you
as if this
were life,
as if
without this
you should go back
to dying.

Persistence

The cicadas trill to be here
after their long sleep.
I sit by a second-story window, open
to summer heat, the smell
of memory. Nothing that happens to us matters,
not even being buried alive for seventeen years,
if we can climb into the trees and sing,
and not stop singing
until we find a mate.

What changes?
The length of hair,
of fingernails,
whatever is of imperceptible growth.
A shaman must have gathered my clippings
to make a smiling doll,
danced and chanted
through many summers,
with an insect's persistence,
until I changed
into a smiling man.

A boy calls down the block for his friends.
I hear the boys who called me
at my window.
I used to think the past
would always call me.
They play until dark,
when the cicadas are silent.
I turn on the light:
the room I have been living in
is bigger than I remember.

Bodies of Water

1.

We walk backward in our fins into
the already amnio-warm spring
water of Hanauma Bay, squat
in the waves and fall
                              into our leggy failure
at limbless grace. You can't swim.
Just float, I say. My one hand on your wrist,
one at your waist, we bend in.

                              You panic after
footholds, knees and shins grating against
coral, stand, spitting out your mouthpiece,
mouth slapped full of water, stammer,
"Did you see them?"

                              Soon, you let go, already
in the rhythm of waves, and I resent
how easily you go. I dive, come up beneath you,
your skin, white underbelly of
an underwater being, and have to touch you,
and lead you
                    to parrot fish, angel fish,
fish yellow in schools of quick cowardice.

Through snorkel and mask, if it is possible to smile,
you smile, believing we are sharing this.
I make my eyes say
                    we are sharing this
and swim away, ashamed of the petty betrayals
that betray my fear
                    that once you see beyond

your terror, you'll see what dazzles there
                              without me.

Out here, unpredictably colored fish
seem to sip, or perhaps kiss, constantly
kiss, the world that holds them, the world that eats them.
Here, no matter how I kick,
I am heaved and dragged by water
that opens out before me, behind me, my huge
defenselessness.

I am afraid
              I will see nothing
beyond my terror
                  of your leaving,
but the knowledge
you will,
because I know we are bodies
of water, hindered in their flow
by skin's little resistance, that this sip
inside our kisses
                  is all we taste
of what flows through us.
I am afraid of how our bodies water
for each other, of how I need
to sip at this
              to keep alive.

2.

Little Shaun drops his diaper, runs
toward the tide pool
                      as if running toward
his mother, bends to embrace it, laughs, so hard
it sounds like choking on water. "Zat?" he asks
of sea anemone. "Zat?" he asks

of everything, wanting its name, his curiosity
ready to laugh
                    at near drowning.

I would be always running naked toward water,
always splashing, but mostly I stand, self-conscious
in my bathing suit, worried by winter fat.
I would be always running toward someone,
discoveries in my hand, asking,
"Can you help me name them?"

Shaun falls. Looks up, startled. It is our panic
that sets him crying, a cry of such force
I fear
        he'll choke on his own water.
                                        I hug
his face to my face, and the water
of my body
            answers his.

3.

The waves are high off the cape
                            of this rocky coast
we had to
            rock-climb
                        down to. Dizzy with heat,
we stand
            ankle-deep in water
                                so cold
the muscles in our arches cramp.
And I remember the cramps that made my legs
lead and pulled me under, how the surface
sealed over my head, and I knew
it was a border between worlds.

As much as the heat
                    makes me ache for it,
I say, it is too cold for swimming. Though
I can't see under, say, it is too rocky
to be safe. Almost everything I've done
I've done
            to be safe.

We dive in,
            are shocked into being
all body.
            Can only stand the shock
                            for an instant,
and run out,
            panting,
                    rubbing each other warm.

Morning Prayer

Call down the stairway after me,
hold me again in your voice,
even uncombed and sleepy eyed,
reminding me we need milk and bread,
you lean out over me
like light, that comes leaning in
summer windows
open toward green
lakes, where dragonflies vibrate
intense as the air between kisses.
Meet me each morning on the stairwell,
in a robe clutched closed at your waist,
newspapers, orange juice, ask me for anything
if I can live in a moment like this.

Okay, So I'm Not Li Po

(But It's Not as if We Were Parted by War; You Were in Florida
Visiting Your Mother, and Anyway, He Was a Drunk)

After three days'
fog and rain,
to awake
to one, high, white, round cloud
running across blue
and blue and blue,
as my heart does
at your return.

Thanksgiving

The morning air tastes of the dark
underside of fieldstones.
Gape-mouthed, milkweed
surrender their last syllables
to November
bracken.
Silver Aspen, White Birch
tremble at the forest edge.
The whole forest is quaking
into light.
A cloud ridge rises
between Pocono
and Kittatinny,
ghost
and smoke.
In a cold wind
dry leaves
hide-and-seek
from ripening
Bittersweet
to dead
Live-Forever.
One more day,
and morning light
will angle
undeniably
toward winter.
But now,
it is the very autumn
of autumn.
What was it?
What I wanted?

At Its Farthest Branch Tip

One bud begins,
as if
to begin,
life needs
small extremes.

I am alive
in small extremes,
in tongue that waters at your mouth,
in this bud that unfolds
toward the life in your body.

The tree, frosted leafless, its bark
wintered hard, comes back.
However stilled,
the water warms and rises,
making most brittle limbs
most pliable.

But when we still,
the blood settles in a bruise
down the length of our bodies,
dark as the underside
of windfall fruit.
And in no April will movement resume.

One winter, when our bones
are lime,
snow weight will break
these burgeoning oaks
we walk under.

Though each blooming
breaks them closer
to that last winter, still,
they bloom.

For even
a little life
is life enough
to blossom.

FIVE

Genesis: A Sequence of Poems

Prologue

The mother of all living was perfect
and happy in her nakedness
before she turned the apple over.
The serpent was a worm in the fruit she bit
to whom her body was only body and
windshook, subject
to the fruit tree's fall.
Seeing the bodiless angels unite
in love, as one spirit, eternal,
she went, in love, for Adam,
and they strained
through their flesh
to become angels.

Their straining only made them
more body.
Jealous of angels, they hated
their flesh; terrified of angels,
whose beauty told them
the garden must reclaim
whatever is not spirit,
they fled, hiding their sex,
hiding the urge that would birth, in sorrow,
new dying,
as if hiding their bodies
they could hide
from death.

I. In the Beginning

Dark with womb water,
he grips your pinky
hard. He won't
let go. His eyes
wander past you, distracted
with light. He tilts
his head, as though listening
for heart shudder. He won't
let go. He must
hold on to you,
creature of air,
to hoist himself out
of his water world.

Your grandfather grips
your wrist, suddenly
strong. Something shudders
against his ears. He won't
let go. Not yet ready
to go back
under the dark water.

The coo and cry of infants,
before they learn
the music of human inflection—
the singing of vowels
through ascending and descending scales
of interrogation and reply—
is whale song.

We are swimmers in air confused
by gravity's drag.
All our dreams and legends of flight:

the memory of weightlessness,
of our amniotic swim,
the memory
of whale grace.

Now your son grips your finger
with his blood-dark fingers
grips his grandson's wrist.
His grandson remembers
how you held onto your father
and learned his fear of water.

II. Bone of My Bones, Flesh of My Flesh

But God, she was more
than everything in the garden.
When she woke, she was all
opening, all reaching:
I thought
she was reaching
for me.

Whatever it was, I
was in the way.
I thought
if I held on hard enough,
pushed back as hard
as she pushed
at me, I could become
what she wanted.
Then
the children came.

The wells I dig never strike
sweet enough water,
and my fingers stink
of marsh mud.
Doesn't she know
I remember
how it was?

If it was all
so perfect,
what was it
she was always reaching for
until she reached
that fruit?

III. She Gave Me of the Tree, and I Did Eat

The night is warm,
a sleeper's breath;
the river bank,
mossed and damp
mons pubis.
Wolf, owl, cricket call:
Love. Love.

The woman wakes
into her lover,
he tastes the earth,
his love, and names
the moment, "Here."
First prays, "Here,
let me live
forever."

And God comes walking
in the cool of the day,
stirs the first wind
that tickles their wet bellies,
tickles them awake
with gooseflesh,
and they know
they are naked.

God asks, "Hast thou eaten?"
Eve looks to her husband, knows
he will lie, fight, beg, die
to defend her, and reaches
for his hand, which is
gone, which is
pointed at her,

and sees his fear
become betrayal, become
sin.

IV. In Sorrow Shalt Thou Bring Forth Children

1.

She lays my palm
where the child in her belly
swims toward birth
as if eager
to get there.

Where?
Here, where we wander
from moment to moment, wondering,
is this the only moment
I am alive in?
Looking for connections
to string our days
into a pattern
we can finger and admire.
Looking for something
older and brighter than who we are,
to offer up our making,
to keep it burning
after our last light closes.

But it is we
who will burn.
The fire does not speak
to us, does not ask or wait
for any offering. It takes.
Makes flesh ash.
Can no more thank
or praise
what it burns
than a flame can
the twig it blackens.

2.

What world would be now
had Isaac fled
or fought his father?
Had Jesus whipped
the Centurions at Gethsemane,
instead of petty merchants
in his father's house?
Abraham's hand was stayed by God
and Christ's torn temple
in three days stood,
but no hand stays,
no Jesus rebuilds,
the bodies singing in formation
to the sacrifice.

There was no time to bury the bodies, no time.
When the shelling stopped
they dragged the dead
to the nearest pit,
threw in dirt, fled
when the shelling resumed,
and in the blasts
the dead rose up again
and pelted the living
with lumps of rotted flesh.

The strongest, bravest, most beautiful youth
was chosen from the tribe and,
dizzy with drums,
disembowled. What shook out
from his belly, shaken out
over the fields.
When the crops came,
red flowers found
between the corn

were carried to his mother as proof
the gods had blessed her loss.

Across the field
where stone crosses flower,
a flag is folded,
a box of ribbons and medals carried
to the dead soldier's mother.

3.

Against my palm,
the future, made flesh,
kicks:
already fighting
to be alive.

To be alive.

If I take you
to the mountain,
to the hill
of skulls,
and bid you gather wood
to build an altar
or a cross;
before I have the chance
to bind you,
even as I promise
that you cannot die,
that you will
arise,
have the courage to defy
or flee
or slay me.

V. Cursed Is the Ground for Thy Sake

The chuck chuck chuck of the hoe
cuts to old, pale soil, turns the new
under, as the son's spring visit ends
with this sharing
of a task.
Work, though not talk,
is better than silence
between them. As their bodies do
what their words cannot,
the son thinks, at least
we are not standing apart.

He hears the quick, raspy whistle
of his father's breath, fears
come morning, he'll be one
sick ache from ankles to neck,
and slows to give him time to rest.
But his father doesn't stop,
and the son knows
this is not a meeting
but a race.

He sees his father as always pouting
his disappointment in sons,
whatever they became for him,
never quite what he demanded they be;
damning them to scurry home
from scoldings by their bosses
as they'd once run from teachers
whose blows told them, as their father's had,
they were lazy, they were dumb,
they would come to nothing;
who bully wives and punish sons

into obeisance, as if mastery of only this—
a woman and a child—
could rein the unnamed fears
that stampede through the dark
like the quick, dim dragons
of childhood.

He looks toward the house,
where his wife and mother
sort iris bulbs,
and every petulant fight
between his father and mother,
him and his wife,
comes sounding the same.
And he wonders if his wife's tenderness
is not the tenderness
of scorn.

She looks at him, questioning,
and waves. He waves back.
Knows, on the long ride home,
he must speak of this; knows,
as always, she will listen
and touch him
as she would
a boy.

VI. But Cain Was a Tiller of the Ground

When my brother mocked me,
called me girl, sissy, fag
because I could not heave the ax,
could not witness the heifer's beheading
and not retch, even as he flicked
drops from his blood-gloved hands
at my hidden face,
I did not stand, did not answer,
but bent myself away,
knowing he, first born, was first
under our father's eye
and first under his anger,
and sorrowed that he turned toward me
what he was too afraid
to turn against our father.

When my brother bullied me,
clubbed to shards
the pots I'd glazed and fired
to carry water to the corn rows,
even as he stomped the dry stalks down, taunting,
no man would do such woman's chores,
I stayed silent, stayed my hand, knowing
he'd mistaken our father's disinterest
for a gentleness toward me,
and had to punish someone
for the gentleness he wanted.

When he came at harvest with his spear,
for the first time called me brother,
and bid I walk with him into the field,
I knew one of us was to be sacrificed.
I heard the earth cry out my name,

and scythed him down, plowed him to pieces,
took his spear, and ran to tell our father
I'd become the son he wanted.

He did not embrace me.
He swung his ax against me
for the killing of his favorite.
The blade just glanced my forehead.
His wild swing made him stumble.
When he looked up at the blood mark
that seeped across my features
and saw I did not blench,
he knew if he ever tried to strike me again
I would kill him,
and said, "Go. Go.
I'll think of something to tell your mother."

VII. And Abraham Built an Altar

Everything had gone as he'd imagined, over and over,
since that night the voice had asked him this.
As always, the boy did not begrudge him anything;
had not complained of the early awakening,
the long trek, the high climb;
had been quick to gather brambles;
had chosen the stone and whet the knife;
had never asked after the missing ram,
sensitive to his old father's dread
of senility.

Now the mourning coo of two dry sticks rubbing together,
and the boy crouched over, patient for the flame, his back
to his father, who tests and retests the hemp in his hands.

He was the envy of all the other fathers
who complained of surly and lazy sons.
His boy was the beauty of all the boys;
the girls in the tribe dreamt of being his.
How could the voice that had promised this son
ask him this? Wasn't it possible this once
it had erred, this once would forgive his doubt?
But this was the voice that had promised him
great flocks, promised him sweet wells, promised him king,
promised him everything he now called his.
He would kill the boy.

VIII. I Have Heard What the Talkers Were Talking

I have heard what the talkers were talking...
the talk of the beginning and the end,
But I do not talk of the beginning or the end.

—Walt Whitman

1.

The dark is just the dark, and yet
passing into sleep
there is this feeling
of passage,
as if the dark were moving, or
something my body moves through.
Falling asleep. Is this the fall
of death?

The old man passes
between dream and remembrance
for months in his hospital bed,
before the last long vigil
when he lets the last breath go.

A bayonet enters the soldier's ribs,
is yanked out, and his life
is yanked out with it,
spirit issuing from a wound
smaller than his lover's mouth.

We think it better to go sudden,
asleep. But to the dying?
How long does it take
from inside the act
to die?

2.

There is something in me, something
not body, that believes
I will never die,
that cannot remember back
to the first fold
creeping across the egg,
pinching it in two,
then four, then eight cells all
deciphering the spiral hieroglyph
of DNA. How does the nucleus know
it will be hair or bone, heart
or brain? Is it something not body
that guides the body through
hydra and sponge, gill and fin,
through bird, webbed feet, mammal?

3.

We lie on our backs
on the beach at night, and,
looking into the stars,
it's easy to imagine
we are eternal.
But what we cannot imagine
is what terrifies us.

The soul in search of salvation
searches for a path
out of the always dying body,
to abandon it, to escape death.
But to abandon the body is
to die.

The hedonist strains
to fuck free of death,
or, if not free, free
to defy, to die laughing,
too drunk to notice
what he flees from, and so
flees life.

We lie on our backs
on the beach at noon
and think, these are such clouds
as God would speak from.
Is it enough
that they are there
and we are here
to see them?
Enough to be alive
in a moment where,
no hand, no hand to strike or save us,
but air and water and sun have hung them?

IX. The Cadence of Vanishing

> *Kiss*
> *the mouth*
> *which tells you,* here
> here is the world. *This mouth. This laughter. These temple bones.*

> *The still undanced cadence of vanishing.*
> — Galway Kinnell

What lives, sings.
Not to defy
the dark,
not to allay
its fear,
but because it is
the dark,
and knowing this knows
it must sing,
for to be alive
is to be a singing thing.

Not the song of longing
for something other
than what is,
it is the song
of being here,
knowing here
is all there is.
An all
that ends.

And, in ending,
gives us more
than mourning,
gives us cause

to sing
that we can sing
while we are here.

If not here, then where?
Where to long for?
Where to go?
Wherever you are
you are going,
will one day
be gone.
And wherever it is
that the spirit goes,
you can't go there.

To wish you could
is to wish yourself
away.
To spend your song
singing your way there,
is to be less
of a singing thing
here.

X. No Angel Is Terrifying

For beauty is nothing
but the beginning of terror, which we are just able to endure,
and we are so awed because it serenely disdains
to annihilate us. Every angel is terrifying.
                              —Rainer Maria Rilke

It is the angels
who are terrified
of us, jealous of us,
who are forced
to live forever
without the kiss
of flesh on flesh,
who pass through one another
carelessly, passionless,
knowing nothing in them changes
from their union.
They are never broken. They believe
in nothing, for belief
is only what stands
after we've been broken.

It is we who believe
with belief so great
we breathed it
into angels, into gods,
having long forgotten
they are images
of what it is in us
that loves
what dies.

Could we hurtle our bodies together forever
we would remain forever

two bodies,
but we have only
this little minute of life,
being departing things,
to hurtle toward each other
whatever it is in us
that is not body.

Because we must die
we must love.
There is nowhere to flee
but toward life,
toward the life in our bodies,
where we are
without death
for a while,
where, for a moment only,
we are angels,
angels of flesh,
perfect and happy
in our nakedness.

Acknowledgments

Grateful acknowledgment is made to the editors of the chapbook, journals, anthologies, and websites listed below, who previously published a number of the poems in this collection, some in earlier versions.

"Casino Pier, Asbury Park." *The Southern Review*.

"Everything I Need to Know I Learned in Kindergarten," and "Hands." *Writing Our Way Out of the Dark* (Queen of Swords Press).

"Everything I Need to Know I Learned in Kindergarten." *Outsiders: Poems About Rebels, Exiles and Renegades* (Milkweed Editions).

"South Mountain." *Bitterroot*.

"Ocean Gate." *Prayers to Protest* (Pudding House Press).

"Ocean Gate" and "On the Boardwalk in Seaside Heights." *Under a Gull's Wing* (Down the Shore Publishing).

"Morning Prayer," "Another Night at the Fights" and "The Pine Barrens." *Paterson Literary Review*.

"Sanctum Sanctorum" and "Persistence." *LIPS*.

"If I Sing." *Pudding House Review*, *Send My Roots Rain* (Paraclete Press), *Writing Ourselves Whole*, *Poetry Wednesday*, and *The Rediscovery Project*.

"And Abraham Built an Altar" and "In Sorrow Shalt Thou Bring Forth Children." *Wordsmith*.

Section Five of *Odd Boy* was previously published in chapbook form as *Genesis: A Sequence of Poems* (New Spirit Press).

The opening epigraph to *Odd Boy* is excerpted from Galway Kinnell's "Flower of Five Blossoms." *When One Has Lived a Long Time Alone.* New York: Alfred A. Knopf, 1990.

The epigraphs to the last three poems in "Genesis: A Sequence of Poems," are excerpted from:

Walt Whitman's "Song of Myself." *Leaves of Grass*, Brooklyn, New York: 1855.

Galway Kinnell's "Little Sleep's-Head Sprouting Hair in the Moonlight." *The Book of Nightmares.* Boston: Houghton Mifflin Company, 1971.

The Selected Poetry of Rainer Maria Rilke. Edited and Translated by Stephen Mitchell. New York: Vintage Books, 1984.

Special thanks to poets Tom Benediktsson, Robert Carnevale, Martín Espada, Maria Mazziotti Gillan, Gregory Orr, Pina Pipino, Sharon Spencer, and especially Reneé Ashley and Dave Caserio for their advice, encouragement, feedback, and friendship; to the faculty, staff, and fellow workshop participants at New York University's Creative Writing Program and the Squaw Valley Community of Writers, especially Robert Hass, Brenda Hillman, Sharon Olds, and, with deep gratitude, Galway Kinnell; to past and present Geraldine R. Dodge Foundation trustees and staff, in particular Jim Haba, Erica Mosner, Wendy Baron, David Mayhew, Lewis Perlmutter, khalil murrell, Bridget Talone, Rebecca Gambale Moeri, Michele Russo, Ysabel Gonzalez, and Victoria Russell, and the countless poets I've met over the years at the Dodge Poetry Festival, for enriching my life and my art; to Bryan Borland for his belief in this book and for helping to bring it into the world; to Seth Pennington for his beautiful cover design; for my siblings Rosemary, Anna, Rich, Kathy, and Dorothy, with love; and to Cheryl Solimini, who is why this book exists.

About the Poet

A native of Jersey City, Martin Jude Farawell has been a landscaper, hardware salesman, cab driver, discount-store manager, graphic artist, actor, DJ, teacher, and visiting artist. He produced several reading series before beginning work as an assistant for the Geraldine R. Dodge Poetry Festival in 1998, which he has directed since 2009. His plays have been produced in off-off-Broadway, college, community, and regional theaters from South Africa to Los Angeles. A graduate of New York University's Creative Writing Program, he has been the recipient of a writing fellowship from the New Jersey State Council on the Arts and a frequent Pushcart Prize nominee. His poems have appeared in the chapbook *Genesis: A Sequence of Poems*, and in a wide variety of journals—*Cortland Review*, *LIPS*, *Literary Review*, *Orion*, *Paterson Literary Review*, *Poetry East*, *Southern Review*, and *Tiferet*, among others—and in a number of anthologies, including *Outsiders* (Milkweed Editions) and *The Traveler's Vade Mecum* (Red Hen Press). He lives in rural Pennsylvania with writer Cheryl Solimini.

MARTINFARAWELL.COM

About the Press

Sibling Rivalry Press is an independent press based in Little Rock, Arkansas. It is a sponsored project of Fractured Atlas, a nonprofit arts service organization. Contributions to support the operations of Sibling Rivalry Press are tax-deductible to the extent permitted by law, and your donations will directly assist in the publication of work that disturbs and enraptures. To contribute to the publication of more books like this one, please visit our website and click *donate*.

Sibling Rivalry Press gratefully acknowledges the following donors, without whom this book would not be possible:

Tony Taylor
Mollie Lacy
Karline Tierney
Maureen Seaton
Travis Lau
Michael Broder & Indolent Books
Robert Petersen
Jennifer Armour
Alana Smoot
Paul Romero
Julie R. Enszer
Clayton Blackstock
Tess Wilmans-Higgins & Jeff Higgins
Sarah Browning
Tina Bradley
Kai Coggin
Queer Arts Arkansas
Jim Cory
Craig Cotter
Hugh Tipping
Mark Ward

Russell Bunge
Joe Pan & Brooklyn Arts Press
Carl Lavigne
Karen Hayes
J. Andrew Goodman
Diane Greene
W. Stephen Breedlove
Ed Madden
Rob Jacques
Erik Schuckers
Sugar le Fae
John Bateman
Elizabeth Ahl
Risa Denenberg
Ron Mohring & Seven Kitchens Press
Guy Choate & Argenta Reading Series
Guy Traiber
Don Cellini
John Bateman
Gustavo Hernandez
Anonymous (12)

Lightning Source UK Ltd.
Milton Keynes UK
UKHW041830281020
372395UK00005B/81